S0-ARS-258

To:

_____

With Love:

_____

Published by Christian Art Publishers
PO Box 1599, Vereeniging, 1930, RSA

© 2020
First edition 2020

Designed by Christian Art Publishers

Images used under license from Shutterstock.com

Scripture quotations are taken from the *Holy Bible*, New Living Translation, copyright © 1996, 2004, 2015 by Tyndale House Foundation. Used by permission of Tyndale House Publishers, Inc., Carol Stream, Illinois 60188. All rights reserved.

Printed in China

ISBN 978-1-4321-3164-7

© All rights reserved. No part of this book may be reproduced in any form without permission in writing from the publisher, except in the case of brief quotations in critical articles or reviews.

22 23 24 25 26 27 28 29 30 31 – 18 17 16 15 14 13 12 11 10

Prayers
FOR MY
BABY BOY

Carolyn Larsen

CHRISTIAN ART PUBLISHERS

God's Precious Handiwork

O GOD,

Thank You for shaping every detail of this precious child within me. You already know everything about this little one.

O Father, surround this child with Your love and protection. This little one, Father, is Yours, not mine but I thank You for allowing me to have the privilege of being his parent.

In Jesus' name,

AMEN.

You made all the delicate,
inner parts of my body and knit me
together in my mother's womb.

PSALM 139:13

KNOWING GOD EARLY

Father,

I pray that this precious little one will come to know You early so he can spend much of his life learning to know You and serve You.

Guide me as I teach him about You. Father, help me be a good model of Your love and care.

Father, don't let me get in the way of him knowing You.
In Jesus' name,

Amen.

You have been taught the Holy Scriptures from childhood, and they have given you the wisdom to receive the salvation that comes by trusting in Christ Jesus.

2 TIMOTHY 3:15

Courage to Try New Things

DEAR GOD,

Father, begin preparing this child for the future by planting curiosity in his heart. Provide opportunities to explore new things as he grows.

I pray that he will have courage to step in to opportunities to use the talents and abilities You have given and that his efforts will bring more awareness to this world of Your love and care.

In Jesus' name,

AMEN.

"Don't be afraid, for I am with you.
Don't be discouraged, for I am your God.
I will strengthen you and help you.
I will hold you up with My victorious right hand."

ISAIAH 41:10

CARING ABOUT OTHERS

Dear Father,

Help me teach my child to remember to be kind and considerate of others. Even as he moves through his younger years when children can be so self-focused, show me how to point him toward generosity and kindness.

Help me model humility as I teach him what it means to be a kind and respectful person who values others' feelings. In Jesus' name,

Amen.

Don't be selfish; don't try to impress others.
Be humble, thinking of others as
better than yourselves.

PHILIPPIANS 2:3

True, Lasting Peace

DEAR FATHER,

Fill my child with peace. I pray that his heart's peace will come from trusting that You hold each day of his life in Your loving hands. Peace comes only from knowing You.

I pray that this precious child comes to understand that and hold onto You early in his life so that his heart will be at peace.

In Jesus' name,

AMEN.

You will keep in perfect peace
all who trust in You, all whose
thoughts are fixed on You!

ISAIAH 26:3

MY HIDING PLACE

O Father,

Protect this boy from all who would try to hurt him, not only physically but also emotionally. Protect him from believing hurtful words. Help me keep communication open with him so that I can encourage Him when he's hurt or lonely.

Most of all, keep him close to You so he always knows he's loved and protected.
In Jesus' name,

Amen.

You are my hiding place;
You protect me from trouble.
You surround me with songs of victory.

PSALM 32:7

God, the Waymaker!

DEAR GOD,

You are the Maker of pathways, the Guide to purpose-filled life. Your Word says You already have a plan for my child's life. Guide his path.

Direct his choices in friends and activities to those who will bring him closer to You and keep him from any temptations to turn away from You.

In Jesus' name,

AMEN.

"I know the plans I have for you,"
says the LORD.
"They are plans for good
and not for disaster,
to give you a future and a hope."

JEREMIAH 29:11

GOD'S CREATIVE POWER

O Lord,

You intricately shaped and formed this new life inside of me. In just a matter of weeks my child's heart was beating and he was already a living being.

Everything his body needs to grow into a complex, active, intelligent adult is already in his tiny body. Every blood vessel. Every muscle. Every cell. O God, You are amazing, and creative.
In Jesus' name,

Amen.

Thank You for making me
so wonderfully complex!
Your workmanship is marvelous -
how well I know it.

PSALM 139:14

Needing God's Help

DEAR FATHER,

I'm holding this tiny human but I do not feel ready for the responsibility of being his parent.

What if I don't know enough? What if I don't have patience? What if I make mistakes? I want to parent him well; to teach him to know You, and to love others. Show me how, Lord. Teach me so I can teach him.

In Jesus' name,

AMEN.

Commit everything
you do to the LORD.
Trust Him, and
He will help you.

PSALM 37:5

A KIND HEART

Father,

I pray this child will develop
a kind heart that looks at others
with compassion.

I pray that he will stand in the gap between
bullies and victims and seek to lift up the
bullied with encouragement.

Father, help him be kind when others
aren't; give of his time and emotions;
consider others more than
he considers himself.
In Jesus' name,

Amen.

Since God chose you to be the holy people
He loves, you must clothe yourselves
with tenderhearted mercy, kindness,
humility, gentleness, and patience.

COLOSSIANS 3:12

God's Promised Help

DEAR LORD,

This child was Yours before he came to my life. I'm honored (and a little nervous) to have the responsibility of raising him. I can't do any of it without You.

Thank You for trusting me with him. Thank You for the gift of him. Help me, guide me and keep me leaning on You, trusting You and following You.

In Jesus' name,

AMEN.

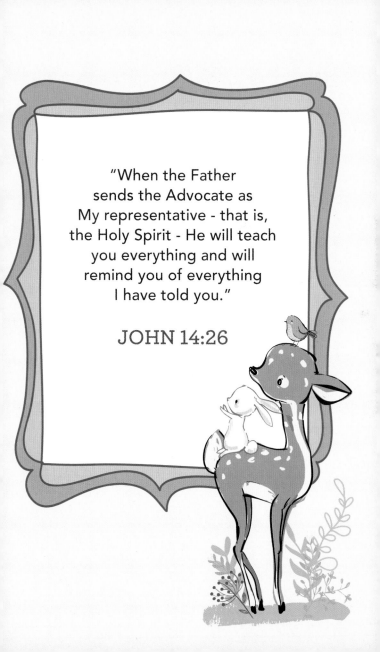

"When the Father
sends the Advocate as
My representative - that is,
the Holy Spirit - He will teach
you everything and will
remind you of everything
I have told you."

JOHN 14:26

MODELING JESUS' LOVE

Dear Father,

From now on every word I speak, every attitude I project will be observed by my child. I want him to know the joy of following You.

Help me remember that his eyes are watching and his ears are hearing. Keep that foremost in my mind so that whatever he sees in me will reflect You to him.
In Jesus' name,

Amen.

Live a life filled with love,
following the example of Christ.
He loved us and offered
Himself as a sacrifice for us,
a pleasing aroma to God.

EPHESIANS 5:2

Encouraging Words

O GOD,

I know I have control issues so I ask You to warn me when I'm trying to control his life. Keep me from stifling the person You want him to be.

Help me encourage his interests even if I don't understand them. Help me enjoy the adventure of him becoming the boy and man You have made him to be!

In Jesus' name,

AMEN.

Let us think of ways to motivate
one another to acts of
love and good works.

HEBREWS 10:24

DEEP, DEEP LOVE

Dear Father,

Even before my baby was born I loved him with all my being. I can't imagine life without him. I'd willingly give my life for him.

I pray that my son will always know that he is deeply, unconditionally loved, by You and by me. May he believe and trust both of those deep loves with no doubts.
In Jesus' name,

Amen.

We love each other
because He loved us first.

1 JOHN 4:19

Never Give Up

DEAR GOD,

I know my child will experience failures, or at least things he considers failure. Those are painful times.

Father, help him discover early in his life that failures are opportunities to learn and grow, not for giving up.

Help him know that failures don't mean the end. Keep him moving forward and learning.

In Jesus' name,

AMEN.

He said,
"My grace is all you need.
My power works best in weakness."

2 CORINTHIANS 12:9

COURAGE TO BE AN INDIVIDUAL

Dear Lord,
Help my son avoid the temptation
to compare himself to his peers.
I pray that he will see his own
uniqueness and embrace it.

I pray that he will not settle for being
one of the look-alike, act-alike pack.
Give him the courage to be himself!
In Jesus' name,
Amen.

I am certain that God, who began
the good work within you, will continue
His work until it is finally finished
on the day when Christ Jesus returns.

PHILIPPIANS 1:6

Send a Good Friend

DEAR FATHER,

I pray my son will cultivate friendships with Christians who serve and honor You. Friends who will challenge him to stay true to You and encourage him to serve You.

I pray for friends who will lift him up when he stumbles and will stand beside him in loyalty and defend him when necessary.

In Jesus' name,

AMEN.

Two people are better off than one, for they can help each other succeed. If one person falls, the other can reach out and help. But someone who falls alone is in real trouble.

ECCLESIASTES 4:9-10

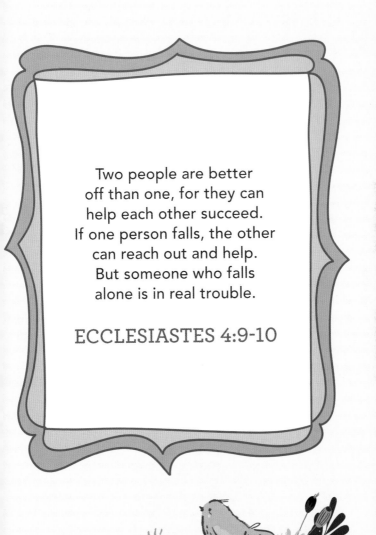

PRAYER FOR FORGIVENESS

O Father,

I long to be a perfect parent but I know I won't be. Father, help my child know that I'm trying. Plant forgiveness in his heart when I'm impatient, critical or selfish.

I pray that my shortcomings will never make him question my love. Give me the courage to admit my failures so that he can learn from my vulnerability.
In Jesus' name,

Amen.

Be kind to each other,
tenderhearted,
forgiving one another,
just as God through Christ
has forgiven you.

EPHESIANS 4:32

Sacrificial Love

DEAR FATHER,

Thank You for this child and the privilege of being his mommy. I don't take it lightly. Having him in my life gives me new understanding of the magnitude of Your love in sending Your only Son to earth for me. What a sacrificial act of love.

Thank You for this child, another evidence of Your great love.

In Jesus' name,

AMEN.

Love never gives up, never loses faith,
is always hopeful, and endures
through every circumstance.

1 CORINTHIANS 13:7

THE
PRIVILEGE
OF PRAYER

Father,

Teach my child the power of prayer.
Help him know the blessing of talking
with You about anything and trusting
that You hear his prayers
and care about them.

I pray he will know the privilege
of sharing in others' lives by praying
for them too. I pray his relationship
with You will grow deeper through
communication in prayer.
In Jesus' name,

Amen.

Don't worry about anything;
instead, pray about everything.
Tell God what you need, and
thank Him for all He has done.

PHILIPPIANS 4:6

Stay Close to God

DEAR FATHER,

Someday my boy may be bombarded by people claiming they know truth – but it won't be Your truth. Guard his heart, Father. May the truths of Your Word take a firm hold in his heart.

Protect him and keep his heart close to You so that he will know real truth.

In Jesus' name,

AMEN.

Come close to God,
and God will come close to you.

JAMES 4:8

BLESSING OTHERS

Dear Father,

Help this child learn that life
is not all about him. Keep him
from being tempted to think that
even the talents and gifts You've
given him are for his own
enjoyment and success.

Show him how to use those
things to serve others and
draw them to You and to enrich their
lives. Give him a helpful heart.
In Jesus' name,

Amen.

God has given each of you
a gift from His great variety
of spiritual gifts. Use them
well to serve one another.

1 PETER 4:10

Lifting Others Up

DEAR FATHER,

Help me teach my child the dangers of comparing himself to others. Help him see the problem of pushing others down in order to elevate himself.

Help me model an attitude of humility and submission to You. Help him become a man who finds his worth in You and because of that can celebrate the successes and joys of others.

In Jesus' name,

AMEN.

"Those who exalt themselves will be humbled, and those who humble themselves will be exalted."

LUKE 18:14

SERVING AND BLESSING OTHERS!

O Lord,

Bless this precious new life with a tender heart filled with compassion for others. Bless him with a spirit that looks for ways to serve and help others. May humility guide him, not pride.

Lord, may he become a man of God who seeks to serve You and those around him. Give him wisdom to know how to do those things.
In Jesus' name,

Amen.

Blessed are those who trust in the LORD and have made the LORD their hope and confidence.

JEREMIAH 17:7

Hands That Serve

DEAR FATHER,

I hold these tiny hands in mine and wonder what this child's future holds. I pray these little hands will be used to serve You. Guide these hands to ways to make life for all on this earth a little better; a little gentler.

Lord, whatever this child's future holds, may these tiny hands be used for big service to You!

In Jesus' name,

AMEN.

Whatever you do or say, do it as a
representative of the Lord Jesus,
giving thanks through Him
to God the Father.

COLOSSIANS 3:17

PROTECT HIS HEART

Dear Father,

Guard this little one's heart.
Protect him from Satan's tricks.
Help him grow into a boy and then a
man who loves You and is submitted
to You in all his thoughts and actions.

I pray that Your angels will be an
army around him, keeping Satan from
him so that as he matures he
will still be choosing You.
In Jesus' name,

Amen.

Stay alert! Watch out for your great
enemy, the devil. He prowls around
like a roaring lion, looking
for someone to devour.

1 PETER 5:8

Making Memories

DEAR LORD,

Help me make memories with my child. Remind me how quickly his young years will pass. Help me push aside things that keep me from making time for him. Help me be creative in how we spend that time.

Help me make time to play and even be silly sometimes so that as he grows he will have wonderful memories of his childhood.

In Jesus' name,

AMEN.

Let all who take refuge in You rejoice;
let them sing joyful praises forever.
Spread Your protection over them, that
all who love Your name may be filled with joy.

PSALM 5:11

DESTINY BY GOD'S PLAN

Father,
I believe You have a plan for my son.
You made him perfect in Your eyes –
just as You planned for him to be.
Thank You that even before he
entered this world, You had
a plan for his life.

I pray, Lord, that he will seek
to follow that plan and be open
to wherever You lead him.
In Jesus' name,
Amen.

"I knew you before I formed
you in your mother's womb.
Before you were born I set you apart
and appointed you as My prophet
to the nations."

JEREMIAH 1:5

Hunger for the Word

FATHER,

I pray that my son will have a hunger for Your Word. I pray that early in his life he will understand the power of Your Word and the benefits to his life of knowing Scripture.

I pray that he will be diligent about hiding Scripture in his heart so that it's always at the ready to help him in his life.

In Jesus' name,

AMEN.

I have hidden Your
word in my heart,
that I might not sin
against You.

PSALM 119:11

BREAKING THE PATTERN

Father,

Our world has become so publicly negative about anyone who holds different viewpoints. Please remind me of this when I'm tempted to jump on the negativity bandwagon. Remind me that little ears are listening.

Help me model kindness so that my child may one day break that pattern by his words and actions; loving others as he loves himself.
In Jesus' name,
Amen.

"Love the LORD your God
with all your heart,
all your soul, and all
your mind. This is the first
and greatest commandment.
A second is equally
important: 'Love your
neighbor as yourself.'"

MATTHEW 22:37-39

Lifelong Trust

DEAR LORD,

Help my son keep his childlike trust in You as he grows up. I pray that he sees Your protection and care in his life and learns that he can trust You to care for him and guide him throughout all his life.

Keep his focus on You so he's not tempted to place trust in anything or anyone else.

In Jesus' name,

AMEN.

Trust in the Lᴏʀᴅ with all your heart;
do not depend on your own understanding.
Seek His will in all you do,
and He will show you which path to take.

PROVERBS 3:5-6

BE STILL

Father,
In this busy, high stress life,
help me model that it's good
to practice stillness.

Give me the vulnerability to be still,
be quiet, be prayerful so that he can
see the value in those actions and
make stillness a practice in his life, too.

Then he will have opportunities
to hear Your voice and know Your
presence in his life.
In Jesus' name,
Amen.

"Be still, and know that I am God!"

PSALM 46:10

Filled with God's Strength

DEAR FATHER,

Fill my child with Your strength. Give him the persistence and endurance to withstand temptations, to stand strong against those who would try to pull him away from his own beliefs and morals, or would discount the value of living for You.

I pray that Your strength in his heart will give him all he needs to stay true to You.

In Jesus' name,

AMEN.

Those who trust in the LORD
will find new strength.
They will soar high on wings like eagles.
They will run and not grow weary.
They will walk and not faint.

ISAIAH 40:31

KEEPING COMMUNICATION OPEN

Father,

Help me keep communication open with this child. Help me listen deeper than his actual words and hear the emotions behind them.

Help me make time to not only hear him but to engage in conversation. If I do that when he's young, the pattern may be established to keep the communication going as he grows.
In Jesus' name,

Amen.

Ears to hear and eyes to see - both are gifts from the LORD.

PROVERBS 20:12

Choosing Joy

DEAR FATHER,

I pray my son learns to be grateful for the gift of life each day. Help him resist being pulled down into negativity through focusing on problems that keep him from seeing daily blessings.

I pray that he sees me start each day with expectation, joy and true gratitude for life and that he will learn to do that, too.

In Jesus' name,

AMEN.

A glad heart makes
a happy face;
a broken heart
crushes the spirit.

PROVERBS 15:13

FOCUSED
ON JESUS

Dear Father,

I pray my son will always keep his eyes on Jesus and that he will learn early in his life to turn to Jesus for guidance, wisdom, comfort and strength.

Help him resist the temptation to push Jesus aside and trust in other people or situations. I pray, Father, that he will stay true to You in his trust and devotion.
In Jesus' name,

Amen.

Oh, the joys of those who do not
follow the advice of the wicked,
or stand around with sinners,
or join in with mockers.

PSALM 1:1

A Good Strong Will

O **FATHER,**

I pray that this child's strong will becomes a strength that helps him be true to himself. May this strength keep him from following a crowd mentality.

I pray that the desire to have friends or to fit in with a crowd will not overpower him. Protect him, Father, through his own strong will.

In Jesus' name,

AMEN.

May the Lord lead your hearts into
a full understanding and expression
of the love of God and the patient
endurance that comes from Christ.

2 THESSALONIANS 3:5

WORRY IS A WASTE OF TIME

Father,

Help my son learn that worry uses up energy and is often about things that he can't control anyway. Help him learn that worry shows a lack of trust in You.

Help me be his teacher on this by modeling trust in You rather than worry. It's not always easy, but with Your help I can be his example. In Jesus' name,

Amen.

"Can all your worries
add a single moment
to your life?"

MATTHEW 6:27

Whatever God Plans

FATHER,

I pray that this child You are forming inside me will be healthy and strong. I pray for physical and mental strength that will lead this child to a wonderful future.

But, Father, if You have something else planned for this child, then prepare my heart to accept it and to trust You with whatever happens because I trust Your love.

In Jesus' name,

AMEN.

You saw me before I was born.
Every day of my life was
recorded in Your book.
Every moment was laid out
before a single day
had passed.

PSALM 139:16

NEVER ALONE

Dear Father,

I pray that my child will know the joy of never feeling alone. I pray for close family relationships, even when we disagree about things. I pray for good friends who will support him and challenge him.

Most of all I pray that he realizes You are always, always with him. Thank You for Your constant presence in our lives. In Jesus' name,

Amen.

"I am with you always, even to the end of the age."

MATTHEW 28:20

Living Worship

FATHER,

I commit to taking my son to church, reading the Bible to him and praying with him. However I know that worship is a heart response to who You are and what You do for us.

I pray that my son will learn to prepare his heart for worship and expect to meet You in those experiences.

In Jesus' name,

AMEN.

I plead with you to give your bodies
to God because of all He has done
for you. Let them be a living
and holy sacrifice—the kind He
will find acceptable. This is truly
the way to worship Him.

ROMANS 12:1

A LIFE DEDICATED TO KNOWING YOU

Dear Father,

Of all the things I could pray for this child, the most important is that he will come to personally know You. I pray that he will give his heart to You at a young age.

I pray that his faith and trust in You will grow stronger and deeper with each year so that his life will be dedicated to serving You.

In Jesus' name,
Amen.

"This is how God loved the world:
He gave His one and only Son, so
that everyone who believes in Him
will not perish but have eternal life."

JOHN 3:16

Parenting with God's Wisdom

DEAR LORD,

Give me Your wisdom in guiding and teaching my son. Give me patience and a sense of humor. Help me appreciate his joy in learning, even when he makes mistakes.

Give me the wisdom to spend time with him because I know these years will go by quickly. Help me be the kind of mom he needs!

In Jesus' name,

AMEN.

If you need wisdom, ask our generous God, and He will give it to you. He will not rebuke you for asking.

JAMES 1:5

CONFIDENT HUMILITY

Dear Father,

I pray that my son will find that sweet balance
between confidence in how You made him
and the gifts and talents You have given him
versus self-pride that pushes others down.
It's a fine line. Guide him in that.

Teach him how to have confidence
mingled with humility and the
strength to lift others up.
In Jesus' name,

Amen.

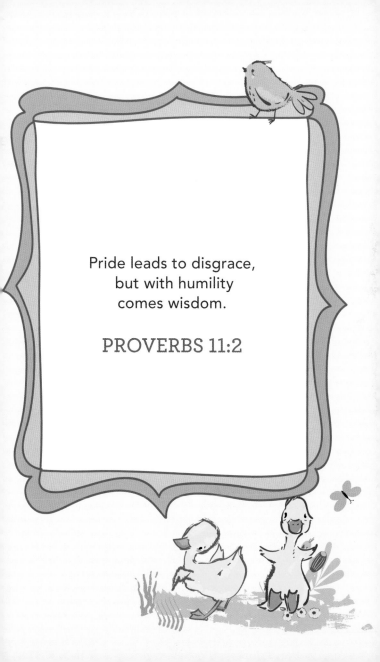

Pride leads to disgrace,
but with humility
comes wisdom.

PROVERBS 11:2

Respect-Filled Fear

DEAR FATHER,

Help my son develop a deep and healthy respect for You. I pray that he will realize that while You do love him, You also have standards, commands and morals which he must obey. Not to obey is sin.

I pray that his understanding of Your Word will grow so that his obedience will grow and that respect-filled fear will keep him obedient.

In Jesus' name,

AMEN.

Fear of the LORD is the
foundation of true wisdom.
All who obey His
commandments will
grow in wisdom.
Praise Him forever!

PSALM 111:10

A GIFT OF LOVE

Dear Lord,

I pray my child will realize how much You love him. Your love is evident in the precious gift of Jesus dying for his sins.

Help him see that he didn't have to do anything to become worthy of that gift. Jesus loved him and died for him before he even knew His name! Help him see His sacrifice of love.
In Jesus' name,
Amen.

God showed His great love for us by sending Christ to die for us while we were still sinners.

ROMANS 5:8